13
2nd *Scroll*

by Thirteen

13- 2nd Scroll
Copyright © 2018 Kirk Scarlett

Edited & Typeset by Jadeen Luke
Artwork by Sara Gonzalez (Esluartes)

ISBN: 978-976-96168-0-6

LIVICATION

To the children of the Sun

ACKNOWLEDGEMENT

Special recognition and gratitude to Rochelle Brown. The spark ignited from your gift of Franz Fanon's "*The Wretched Of The Earth*" continues to blaze unyieldingly the Pan-Afrikan spirit of Liberation.

Sincere appreciation to Jadeen Luke for your beautiful soul and much valued and essential editing and typesetting.

Heart of love to Sara Gonzalez (Esluartes) for your priceless art work.

Salute to Sis. Mitzie, Miguel Lorne, The 2003 Rastafari Global Reasoning and all the ones who have been and continue to be guiding stars.

Love and thanks to the ancestors for constant inspiration and reference.

CONTENTS

3^2

YOUTHS REUNITING WITH THEIR ROOTS

FOREWORD

I Nation has chosen to fight the systemic breakdown of the true nation of the sons and daughters of the Diaspora with the most effective tool against ignorance - Knowledge. There is an urgency in these cries and decrees made in this work. Over and over the themes are addressed, reworked and posited from different perspectives, but remain essentially the same.

The work represents a plea from the depths of the post-colonial self, to know itself and actualize. Siting oppression not as a hinderance but a catalyst. The cry for awakening is loud and clear, and I Nation has been sounding this declaration since he first decided to change the course of Jamaican popular culture by empowering a generation with literature that was intentionally banned and repressed in Jamaica.

With his words sounds here he has now consolidated the sentiments of historical, metaphysical, socio-political and philosophical texts into a palatable and thought-provoking collection that can now be accessed by even those who would refuse to research and study for themselves.

"I told them the Pope is Satan the devil" is a clear indication of the unapologetic nature of these unfolding pages.

Listen carefully students of all ages.

Jah 9 (Janine Cunnigham)

INTRODUCTION

The term revolutionary has been mis-interpreted, mis-used, and mis-understood. The revolution will not be led by a person but a collective leadership of person(s). These revolutionaries will have an evolved psyche, whose form of rebellion is not guns and bombs but their 'livity'.

I -Nation is the exemplification of a revolutionary in our times, choosing the unbeaten path, enduring the struggles, ridicule, and heartache as those before him, who have tried to liberate the minds of their people. His tool to fight the oppressor is the circulation of literature, books, text, and manuscripts that are not available at library nor studied in schools, yet vital to the liberation of the enslaved African mind.

I will be forever thankful to I-Nation, for it is he who exposed me to the works of C.L.R James, Steve Biko, Franz Fanon, Amos Wilson, John Henrick- Clarke, J.A. Rogers, Chancellor Williams, and Cheikh Anta Diop. For years, I-Nation has been distributing the thoughts of others and now it is his time to distribute his own thoughts to the world through his collection of writings called 13.

13 the 2nd Scroll is compilation of historical analysis and social commentary not just of Jamaican society, but issues plaguing the down-pressed and disenfranchised across the world. In, '*Liberty Lays With Garvey*', I- Nation critiques the use of mass-media to indoctrinate the masses, "*World plantation, minds shackled, and hearts chained...Media whips all inline... Government makes humane a crime.*" In '*Glory of Heaven and Earth*' I-Nation warns about the

idea of technological advancement that are actually detrimental to the people, "*From a card to a chip that how it all begins.... Card here to overcome inconvenience... beware it becomes an inconvenience...Behold this tiny little chip... In your wrist or wherever you choose to have it... Now you can't lose it...Suicide or homicide to try and remove it... Property of the Government... All rights to key and kill switch*" I- Nation also delves into spirituality - 'Nyahbinghi' and power and beauty of love between a man and woman in 'Together Forever".

This book is a must have for those concerned with the plight of the African people of the world, those trying to escape mental slavery, and those wanting to learn the tricks of the orchestrators of the system we live in. I- Nation has managed to simplify complicated sociological, economic, and psychological theories, into a language that the masses will understand. This work has the proper title 13 '2nd Scroll' for it is a manuscript that will be referenced throughout the ages.

Give thanks brother I-Nation, it's a bold and most welcome contribution to our enlightenment.

Strength to strength,

Linton Hinds Jr
I Never Knew TV

HANNIBAL-GARVEY

I told them there's no Alps
Rightly you did
I showed them there's no alps for their will or their unity
Truly you did
Was a beautiful sight
You were the terror of Rome
Only in your likeness, Your Greatness
Your confidence was my alter
I taught them of it
I told them that with it they have won even before the start
Without it, they are twice defeated
You've served true and greatly, Your Greatness
One day they'll all be swept up in your whirlwind

POST-RACIAL

Too much 'black stuff'.
Too much talk of Afrika.
Forget the past and come together.
Post-racial the game,
All got to play.
A new day massa say,
What do you say?
Are you game or are you in dismay?
Does one race still bear the pain while another ever in gain?
Supremacy or reciprocity?
What's the ideology of this post-racial reality?
Security or calamity?
Identity or identified?

RACE FIRST

Race First.
No, not racism
Just the righteous duty of securing home
Be of genuine value to self first, then of greater worth
to neighbour
It is inherent and just
Unwise to not concur
The unwise say it's folly, all race must come together now
The wise knows intra precedes inter
Dance a yard before yuh dance aboard
If you master not your own unity then how will you fair in
the grand assimilation?
Will you not become victims of circumstances and powers
you don't wield?
How do you spend before you own a purse?
Race First is life first - plain and simple.

SMELL THE COFFEE

Chairman Mao took Garvey's "Race First" philosophy and
turn China a world Super Power
Today China considers it their right to own
Garvey's homeland
It is sacred and holy ground
The people are gold
Their culture – oil, and their trust - diamond
Very high in demand
The world's fastest man
The world's greatest Legend
The world's only Livity
Who to be in authority?
Euro/Euro-America or China or "Afrika for Afrikans...-
those at home and those abroad"?
Why you think you have the best brew?
Wake up and smell the coffee J.A. - ***RACE FIRST***

LIFE! LIVE IT OR LEAVE IT
(rep. Killa Roach)

Life! Live it or leave it
Western Civilization turn it into a laboratory
Self-experimentation
Personal scientists
Seeking serenity in insanity
Civility in barbarity
Humanity in savagery
Renaissance of criminality
Odyssey of ignoring balance
Death industry and victim ideology
Divine response!
Afrikan response!
Now! Without hesitance

KILLA ROACH! DEMUS! MILLER! FORTH STORAGE! DENHAM
TOWN! ZION TRAIN! WEST KINGSTON!
TIVOLI GARDEN! JIM BROWN! JAH T! BAG A BAUGH! CHRIS
ROYAL! CLAUDIE MASSOP! PRESIDENTIAL CLICK! PRESIDENT
DUDOS! WEST KINGSTON! EVERY INNER CITY! EVERY GARRI-
SON! EVERY GHETTO! EVERYBODY! EVERY SOUL! ANCESTORS!
UNBORN! TO BE BORN!
MARCUS GARVEY! TACKY! NANNY! PAUL BOGLE! SAM SHARPE!
JOEL ROGERS! JOHN HENRIK-CLARKE! LEONARD HOWELL! BOB
MARLEY! BURNING SPEAR! PETER TOSH! BUNNY WAILER!
QUEEN IFRICA! SIZZLA KALONJI! CAPLETON! REGGAE! RASTA-
FARI! PAN-AFRIKANISM! MARIJAUNA! BLACK WOMAN! BLACK
CHILD! BLACK MAN! BLACK GOD! BLACK TIME!

STARDUST SPARKS

To shoot an arrow, you got to bend a bow
Life is much more than the Five Kings know
Cannot hit the mark under their control
Got to reign them in
Tithe the Prince of Peace
Arise evolved
Worthy of the seven-seal trod to greet the Conquering Lion
Every roar is a triumph
Unearthing the Basic Instructions Before Leaving Earth
Bow bend and arrow hits its mark
Living is practice and accuracy the chart
Will in charge
Stardust sparks

GONG-TUFF GONG

I told them the Pope is Satan, the Devil
Their religion a smoke screen to keep the people in
ignorance of truth
Rightly you did
I told them I feel like bombing a church now that I know
the preacher lying
I also told them I shot the sheriff but I didn't shoot the deputy
Justly you felt and acted
You were the Psalms - high and in demand
Sun of the Conquering Lion
Rastafari mission and Reggae weapon
Truly a Legend, Your Greatness
Only in your likeness, Your Greatness
Tuff like the Gong
Babylon and its false organizations and hypocritical system
must go down!

MANLEY-BUSTAMANTE

I gave them the National Workers Union and
the People's National Party
I gave them the Bustamante Industrial Trade Union and
the Jamaica Labour Party
Together, Independent Jamaica, heroic works we have done
Heroic and knightly, only you throw away your
knighthood for Federation?
Mr. Rhode Scholar, you ought to know better
If unity was the mandate, why Hon. Marcus and his
U.N.I.A. and P.P.P. so grave a threat?
Why Gong Howell and his Rastafari Pinnacle such a menace?
No unity for one island, much less unity of multiple islands
You think Massa would just let it pass?
Say what you may, I still believe in the Federation
Unity isn't the danger, only the ideology that harnesses
and sustains it
Mine wasn't of the Pan-Afrikanist or ecclesiastical ideal as
Gong Howell or Hon. Garvey
It was no different than yours, only more ambitious...

to be cont'd

SOVEREIGNTY

Emancipation!
Slavery end but first a period of apprenticeship
Forty hours per week without pay or just call it
minimum wage
One and the same
Illegal but structure remains
Plantation still the name
Society of slaves
Emancipation still fleeting from reality but permanently
affixed to calendar
Every year is celebration and parade
Compensation 'holy day'
Proud 'boasie' slaves
Remove the kinks from your brain and return them to
your hair
Go discover Garvey and find yourself at the right side of
The Almighty

CURE OF HAM

What did Ham do wrong?
Why curse his children?
Was he to do as his brothers and remain calcified?
No pine eye to see nakedness and know truth
Only quick to defend lies and cover in deception
Looking out of self for sovereignty
He didn't choose it, yet his children cursed with it
Servants of their uncles Eagle and Dragon
Welcome the Conquering Lion
Give thanks for His visit
Now the pride roars...from Canaan to Judah
The curse was a misfit...best try the pig
Black Kush so pure the sun loves to kiss

H.A.M.

Uncle Sam is Ham still cursed?
Have not his children served you richly and faithfully?
Made and keeps you The super power
Centuries of unimaginable, unparalleled terror and damnation
Yet they cling to you like a suckling to mom's breast
Will you ever give them rest?
Will you take your heel from their neck?
Mighty Europe haven't you had enough?
So much blood, sweat and tears
So many bodies, so many souls
Do you really think you will have the last laugh?
Great China, what more must we offer?
Betrayed Afrika, H.A.M. bears no blame, pineal is the sight
to obey

to be cont'd

NO GUNS

When our grandfathers had no guns
Thy Kingdom come
Thy will be done
On Earth as it is in Heaven
Walking gods
Moving mountains
Alive pyramids
Roaring vision
Glorious manifestation
Timeless realization
Forward ancient iration
Our grandsons shall have no need of guns
Ancestors' kingdom come

WALKING SUN

When our grandfathers had no guns
Ignorance wasn't gold
Knowing self, the only crown
No vile to the lance
Fair and balance
No reptilian disturbance or mammalian interference
CC divine rating
No separation only variation
Love - the levitation and peace - the configuration
Tree of Life not Treaty of Lies
Christ not Christians
Walking Sun not son with gun
Up and onward to reclaiming the way of our grandfathers

3^2

LIBERTY LAYS WITH GARVEY

Is it real or is it all staged?
CNN the hero
Evidence from ground zero
Slavery in the twenty-first century
Sad and surprised
Grieved and angered
Hashtags and demonstrations
Libya the failed state?
Did they murder Gaddafi to reinstate slavery?
Arabs selling Blacks for Euro and the mighty US dollar
What's the cause, who's at fault?
Arabs wrong, Blacks just damned or all according to a plan?
What cause Blacks to leave their homeland seeking
salvation in foreign lands?
Bottleneck in Libya waiting to sail across to the saviour
Arabs unable to fulfil their agreement of getting them over
Opportunity or calamity?
Refugees or merchandise?
Auction blocks not assistance for Blacks
A global fact, but Libya got caught in the trap
Another headline to the fact
Heaviest burden is still being Black
Grave enemy still white supremacy
Great industry still slavery
World plantation, minds shackled, and hearts chained
Media whips all in line
Government makes humane a crime
Crabs in barrel or puppets on string?
Grinding slow but grinding still

Sad to see but who's really looking?
Eyes socialized for the net to work
On forward but still in reverse
Stuck in a western hearse
Libya the rehearsal to revamp their purse
Watch out for the outburst
From Tripoli to Tivoli, slavery in the twenty-first century
Liberty lays with Garvey
Blacks fail to whirlwind his philosophy
Still phantoms of his opinions
Hooked on apple though the taste remains onion

CHILDREN LIVE WHAT THEY LEARN

He who spares the rod hates his child,
The bible doesn't lie
Spare the rod and spoil the child,
Timeless warning of the wise
Corporal punishment a crime,
Government so nice
Parents and teachers leave the child let him spoil
Nice government will deal with him in due time
Iron bars and flying bullet
No rod spared
He must behave
Children live what they learn,
So who's really to be blamed?
Government educates him, and media inspires him
Parents and teachers worry for him
Where did he learn all these things?
Government will do the interrogating
The charging, prosecuting and executing
Media eulogize the whole thing
A Ponzi scheme
Every child a hedge fund
Government milks parents like cash cows
Abuse teachers like mawga dog
 Government the star like dividend
He controls all evidence, no worry of a bank run
Media lets go of the question mark
Say he's long been the constellation of the matrix
From the womb to the tomb
All in-tune
Everyone his balloon

Burst or inflated, he keeps all up to date
Desire - the route he pervades
Will - he eats all day
The matrix runs without delay
Child sway from spoil to rotten
Parent pray all sins be forgotten
Teachers brace for the worst to happen
Nation cowers under the stench
Government and media say it's their preferred aroma
Kabaka says it's a suffocation
Revolution the only liberation
Government and media got to be overpowered
Rescue the child and save the nation
Empower the parent and heal the nation
Honour the teacher and enrich the nation
No more damnation
Government and media redesigned to be the board and
not the chalk
Now they can truly be of service
No sweet talk, simply walk the walk
No child led astray or provoked to wrath
No parent stressed all day or think they've failed
No teacher feels dismay or out of place
No more rat race
Solidarity and prosperity no longer a maze or phase
Collective security divinely engaged
Children live what they learn

SANKOFA IN FULL ORDER

Ghetto youths, the world is against you but, cannot do
without you
Keep standing tall and rise above all cause
You're the best of the earth and it's a heavenly truth
It's one big Ghetto
The world can't get nuh better than you
New world got to be designed by you
Still Kabbalah Stone, head cornerstone
Hiram Abif learned it all from you
From the science of the square & compass to the beauty
of the ankh & sceptre
Ghetto youths, you are the bloodline of the Creator
Another pyramid can't be built without you
The tools and the secrets lie within you
Throw away the gun, it is only there to distract you
Given to confuse you
Turn your roar into a bark
Best-friend wearing a cross
They laugh while you skylark
Turning cemeteries into parks
Wretched and heartbreaking
Ghetto youths no more partaking
Rainmaker awakening
Time to shower in ancestors' blessings
From Kingston to Addis AbaBa
From New York to AccRa
From Montego Bay to the Big World Ghetto
Every ghetto youth, it's up to you
One hundred forty-four thousand crystals await
your response

Five Kings longing for you to reign them in
Crown you 'Prince of Peace'
Geez the word speaks
The sound echoes from the east
The power within all who seek
Seals released, Conquering roar
Pine high and summum bonum stoned
Creator mode, creation zone
New Flower takeover
No to their NIDS
No dawn for their New World Order
With robots becoming citizens,
All mankind got to come together
Watch out for the clones
Beware Order 66
Execution is promised
Who dares to have their name on the list?
Jibo, you are not a member of the family
Sophia, humanity needs not your help with the creation
of the future
Artificial Intelligence is Darth Vader
Skywalker will not be overpowered
Only love can save love
No greater power at any hour
Life is before death and after
No fear of the crumbling of matter
Eternal is the joy that follow
Spiritual is the intelligence to null & void all horror
The blueprint we never borrow
Ghetto youths the ink is in your marrow
Let it flow and vanquish all terror
From Project Stardust to Death Star Battle Station to
Starkiller Base
What a fate?

Ghetto youths, you're destiny's date
Galactic war internal or externally waged?
World Leaders, what's your response?
Will you ever make a humane decision?
Allow love a beautiful day
Let the moment never go away
No weapons, no destruction
No exploitation, no retaliation
No ignorance, no arrogance
Reciprocity & balance
Ghetto Revolution
New Flower manifestation
Ma'at fertilize the land
Heru becomes all dons
Anuk Ausar the ambition
Eleven Laws
It never began at one
Forever beyond A.I. comprehension
Ashkenazi vs. Nazi dreaded realization
Eternal is the peace of man
Amen ends all faults, is the end of all wrath
Sacred is the craft of the science of heart
World Leaders you are criminally charged
For deception and fraud
Lies and denials of all sorts
Death and damnation without remorse
Destruction and suffering without cause
Divine is the obedience not the law
Man "Know thyself" is the only command
Sizzla Kalonji sounds the alarm
Born and raise in a di Ghetto Revolution
Proper Education is da solution!
Proper Education is the solution
Proper Education is the solution!

Know thyself, there's no more proper education
Behold the universe within
No more fairytale, no more make-believe
World Leaders no more extension on your lease
Of all powers you're relieved
New Flower's fragrance perfuses your defeat
Your droids wont attack, they will retreat
No to your electronic persons
No Frankenstein's Monster to the New Flower
Obi-Wan Kenobi cut down the chosen
The battle is internally won
No victory with gun in hand
All prodigal sons must return home
Force within never grows old
Always ready to heed command
Every ghetto becomes Tehuti's school
Thrice great the golden rule
From Ori your divine root to Orishas your creation tools
to your Neteru of justice & truth
Sankofa in full order
Rastafari ites the ancient banner
God within answer all prayers
Ghetto youths to the rescue
The world welcomes its Saviour...

GLORY OF HEAVEN AND EARTH

All know it's not a joke but love to believe it's a real joke
Government the noose around our throat
Tighter it gets, the more we vote
In this administration we place our hope and dreams
Next election we'll deal with our wants and needs
Cycle proceeds
We grieve but we concede
No revolution to disturb the peace
Many loud barks but no teeth to inflict defeat
Government so pleased
We should be flying but they love to see us creep
Say caterpillar is easier to keep
Manipulate and make believe
Amusement for nourishment
Mercedes for excellence
Violence for security
Terror for assurance
New law passed according to plan
Our welfare never at hand
Only rights confiscated one by one
No right to say no or take a stand
No right to have any rights
Violence so polite
Seems it happened overnight
Welcome to the New World Order
Utopia veil failed
Dystopia seized the hour
Why did it have to come to this?
Quarantined to "make clean"
Chipped and programmed

Cyborgs and droids
Aliens and zombies
Avatar and last breed
At war or at ease?
Matters not
It's a world that ought to remain on the screen
No joke or make-believe
Noose got to be removed if we will to make it not real
From a card to a chip that's how it all begins
Card here to overcome inconvenience
Beware it becomes an inconvenience
Behold this tiny little chip
In your wrist or wherever you choose to have it
Now you can't lose it
Suicide or homicide to try and remove it
Property of the Government
All rights to key and kill switch
For now, it's just for the basics
Identified and taxes
Watch out for the upgrade
Thought & behaviour
What to do and what not to say
Order is the game played
New world, same old noose
Cut away now for you know these words bear truth
There's an alternative to the noose
Government can truly be of use
Just the ideology they chose
No more exploitation & victim
Welcome cultivation and enlightenment
Man is divine, earth is alive and government loves to see us
take flight
Say butterfly is a more beautiful sight
Metamorphose and make real

Truth for nourishment
Peace for excellence
Justice for security
Love for assurance
One law passed, to "Know Thyself"
Our welfare always at hand
All rights uphold
Man's upgrade strictly spiritual, not artificial or virtual
Earth's care strictly reciprocal, not partial or parasitical
Peace so loud it resounds
Eternally abound
Pineal vision
Conquering Lion decision
Five Kings submission
Everyone's ambition
No denial or inhibition
Man's only resolution
We all gonna sing the same song
Is Ra El?
Wrestle with God and prevail a god
Vibration in accordance with Earth and Heaven
Man, the balance of glorification
Ignorance, the devil of confusion
Confusion of what or who is man?
Purpose and master plan?
Government the answer
To organize and centralize a solution
No deviation
No power-hungry exploitation
Purely committed to revelation
Truth latent within everyone
Force strong within but it's your decision
Will you be a tool or will you be a weapon?
Will you be confused or will you reckon?

Land were the gods love to be
Ethiopian stretch forth your hand
Mysteries revealed
Instructions adhered
All in good care
Love the word, truth the sound, justice the power
Government in ancestor gear and
citizens the glory of Heaven and Earth
Time to unearth and be aware

KING OF THE ANIMAL KINGDOM

Civilizations come and civilizations go
Nations rise and nations fall
Gods reign and gods perish
Homer the cause and also the effect
On his name you should put some respect
He lives for the fame
Matters not what it takes
Lies or genocide
He makes the rules
He says when its true and when it's a crime
From grave robbing to moon walking he seeks no pardon
He'll boldly go where none has gone before
He's the final frontier
On him the sun will forever stare
Matters not he's not kissed for its glare
So unfair
He swears
His wrath got to bear
Sun kissed neck under his heel
He's the Man, the real deal
All before him was primitive
Put some respect on his name
From Alexander the Great to Trump the President
He runs all residents
Matters not he's a pestilence
Democracy and advancement
No mercy, no remorse
All resources to the port
Laugh it off in All Inclusive resorts
Put some respect on his name

He lives for the fame
Look at the world he creates
Matters not the price paid
He bears no shame
Know he's lost but says he found a way
Silly game he plays
The end he'll do anything to delay
Who dares have a say?
He's armed to the grave
In a galaxy far away, he'll start a new day
Do you dear to have a say?
Tell him there's no getting away
You executing the brave psychiatrist's diagnosis
His game has finally ended
You avoiding with all possible speed
Leave him to run headlong in the abyss
He was and is wrong, his cabal still missing one
Forever stuck at man
Delaying divine plan
Those before was on an evolution trod
Gods they worshiped were no more than the awakening of
latent faculties within self
Ether Kingdom behold but with fury he caused
a new beginning
Man! King of the Animal Kingdom
Put some respect on his name
From Darwin the species king to Bill Gates the billionaire
to Monsanto the GMO king
From Caesar the conqueror to Obama the pacifier
Two millenniums Man of the Year
The third beholds his final gear
The fourth has nothing to fear
Just need to stay clear
Don't get caught in his flare

Beware!
Dying hour awakes grave power
So sweet before the sour
So social for the net work
Chipped for net worth
Indebted before birth
A bottle a water is an empty purse
Never knew living but now surviving shelters in a hearse
Just yesterday you were tweeting and lost in mirth
Today plight overruns earth
Never knew it could get much worse
A curse but he's not be blamed
Put some respect on his name
From Samuel Colt to Mark Zuckerberg
From Mr. Thistlewood to Sir Henry Morgan
Killed for your organ
The market high in demand
Melanin ten times the price of gold
Supremacy unfolds
Truth runs out of clothes
Inferior is his bow
Love of power its arrow
Terror & horror
Power of love foreign to his marrow
Calcified hollow
Lookout and be ruled
Divided his tool
Clever and crude always his mood
No excuse
Put some respect on his name
From Cecil Rhodes to Ralph Lauren
From Baron to Duke
From Archbishop to Pope
He's the great white hope

He bears the burden
From primitive to New World Order
Knows he's out of order but who dares to put him in order
God long been his partner
Kill his son and resurrect him the Saviour
Who don't believe shall burn in hell fire
Matters not that he's a liar
Just have faith and say a prayer
He has all the answers
Matters not their side effects
Disaster on disaster
Apologise and then back to laughter
No wrath for him to take cover
All his sponsor
The universe is mental and he holds the trigger
Who will unplug and abyss his matrix?
Forsake his flock and stop his clock?
Get him from soul and off your back
No more mind games or heart attack
Free to return to the trod of rising the sun within
A rude interruption, a bad habit, all to the abyss
Put a eulogy on his name and delete him from scene

ONE

Don't be a spoke
We been travelling before the wheel
Time and distance didn't impede
Neither mountains or seas
Like the breeze we moved as we pleased
Rise in the east and set in the west
Every day, we took no rest
The earth is the fullness and we were the gods thereof
Now where are we at?
Whose wheel and where's it heading?
What load is it carrying?
Too much talking
Walls hearing
No bargain
Get off or continue rolling
Where's it heading?
No one knows, only it won't stop without a crash
Waiting on the jackpot or you disembarking and seek
rescue like Lot?
Pay tithe like Abram
Omnipresence the Prince of Peace
Once more travelling like the breeze
Omniscient and omnipotent unleashed from within
Greet Mwalimu Garvey in the whirlwind and welcome the
new beginning
Pyramids constructing
Ancestors smile and posterity sings a song the victory
finally won
Now all truly one

NYAHBINGHI

From Black River to Blue Mountain
Of your treasure there's no end
Straighten any bend
Free the lion from the den
Roar to heaven
Who you are, what you got, how you give,
Remarkably unparalleled
Pencil turns to pen
Eternity into a moment
Life in the now
Serendipity abounds
Talk of the town in every nation on the globe
None dispute or oppose
Water any hose
Once dead now aroused
No cat and mouse
Lion and lioness pride up
Fill all cups
Of you there's not enough
Got to behold what you possess
Relinquish all stress
A nest of what's best
Carried beyond land and ocean just for your potion
A lotion to permeate comfort and repel commotion
High grade emotion
Blue mountain brewed and Black River steamed
Take hold and reign supreme
Nyahbinghi, you are the only true Queen

TOGETHER FOREVER

Nothing changes but the weather
My love stays forever
Sunshine or thunderstorm, fair or inclement
My love will stand the test
You deserve nothing but the best
I give nothing less
All challenges the unleash of greatness
If I'm the head then you're surly the neck
Without you on the platter like John the Baptist
Truer love has never been practised
Two whole, not halves but our oneness can't be passed
If you are the heart then I'm the beat
Your joy is all I seek
Karma free and complete
Never leak or deplete
Blissful without condition
In harmony I hold your hand
In matrimony you keep me a God
No wrong committed to secure your praise
If I'm the master then you are the plan
Fulfilling your command for your love I was born
Fire from the Gods to keep you warm
Water from the rock to quench your thirst
The power of my love knows no hearse or purse
Eternal like change, nothing changes but the weather
Together forever...

GALACTIC DATE

She gave birth to life and he was satisfied
Worshipped her all night
Work until daily light
When the sun rise, she was surprise
Most marvellous sight
Conquering Lion and the Divine Virgin looking on eternity
Beholding its wonder and praise
Their love will never be replaced
She was truly amaze
Nile flow from her eyes all day
Blue and white runneth they
Inundate creation clay
Presented him and say it's his for play
He was truly amaze
To work, he didn't hesitate
His best play
Kemet black clay
Black Kush
Guardians of the Highway
Masons of the Pyramid
Ankhs of Light
Shineth to all lands
Civil and balance
Empire and nations
Community and individuals
All sing their praise
Pilgrimage to look upon her face
Obedience to roar his name
She was truly amaze
Kissed him and said: My God, you are truly great

He held her and said: My Love, by you and for you,
I'm powerless without your grace
Let's take leave of this place
I feel guilty with all my work & play,
I haven't been giving you my undivided attention
What say another galactic date?
Man must face his fate
Heru will set him straight, ever they misbehave
Right now, I just want to look upon your face
Hold you like it's our last embrace
As we go on this galactic date, wandering what beauty awaits...

YOUTHS REUNITING WITH THEIR ROOTS

TO OUR BELOVED STUDENTS

Our first National Hero, His Excellency, The Most Hon. Marcus Mosiah Garvey, taught us that "*the man who is not able to develop and use his mind is bound to be the slave of the other man who uses his mind...*", and so it was for almost four hundred years Throughout chattel slavery we, Afrikans, were restricted from developing and using our minds. Our physical prowess of working the plantations and securing wealth for Master and Europe was our only good fortune.

Many of our ancestors shed blood or lost their lives for simply touching or going so far as to look into a book. Their only education was terror - perpetual and merciless suffering - to recognize and accept their fate as slaves. Emancipation brought change; no longer a criminal offence, education became a novelty, a well sought-after treasure for all Afrikans. Unfortunately, the treasure was not to be found in the places provided. In the words of the great Pan-Afrikan scholar and author John Henrik-Clarke, "*Powerful people cannot afford to educate the people they oppress ... because once you are truly educated, you will not ASK for power you will TAKE it.*" With this in mind it is clear that the education provided by the former slave masters turned colonial masters, is not in favour or in the best interests of Afrikans-enslaved, now colonial subjects.

The education and schools were actually designed to perpetuate subservience to Europe and the inculcation of a complex based in inferiority and hatred of self (of Afrika and being Afrikan). The placing of the shackles removed from wrists and ankles, replaced with mind and heart. If, as our first National Hero teaches, "*education is the medium by which a people are prepared for the creation of their own particular civilization, and the advancement and glory of their race,*" then, beloved students, there is no way under the sun that the oppressor will afford the oppressed true education. The innocent tool of cultivation that education is, had to be transformed into a treacherous weapon of exploitation: a miseducation, social engineering, indoctrination into imitating Europeans and being proud subjects of European thought & behaviour. Independence brought little change, the mental enslavement continued; the indoctrination into being anything but ourselves - anything but Afrikan - continued. Our Independent leaders did not see it fit to have us recover from the horrors of slavery and colonialism to reclaim our origin, truth, education, wholistic way of life, or our Afrikan identity and power. Their concern was, and still is, to make us as compliant as possible to further an ongoing exploitation.

The Pan-Afrikan ideal of our ancestors and National Heroes- Sam Sharpe, Queen Nanny, Paul Bogle, Marcus Garvey - betrayed and disregarded by neo-colonialist. These neo-colonialists are those who have no vision beyond the fulfilment of a mandate of us being '*a tree without root*' - a people of a colonial history, slave origin and an exploitive culture. It is sad but it is the truth, beloved students; from chattel slavery to colonialism to this here neo-colonialism, our leaders continue to be our enemy. Still that is not the worst. The worst is having us become our own worst enemy, so much so that even schools become garrisons in need of metal detectors and police security, certainly this is not yours or any other students' fault.

The emperor of Ethiopia, H.I.M. Emperor Haile Selassie I

teaches that "*Young people will be young people. You can't change the uncouth manners of the young...The young don't know what they want...They can't know it because they lack experience, they lack wisdom...It is for the head of the state to show the young which path to tread.*" Our heads of state and the successive governments have failed miserably at providing a righteous path for you, students, and the young people of this nation to tread safely and triumphantly. Sankofa is that long forsaken righteous path, beloved students, we must return and reclaim that which has been lost in order to move forward triumphantly. You must go beyond colonialism and slavery, beyond white supremacy and western civilization to our own grand Afrikan civilization, our own heritage and reclaim your Afrikan identity. An identity with roots as deep and old as earth herself. With such an identity you can't help but be powerful, you can't help but lead triumphant lives, you can't help but be princes and princesses; identity is key, beloved students.

The shallow Jamaican identity is incapable of making you whole, sound and powerful. The whole, sound and powerful of the island are those who have not forsaken or denied their original identity and heritage. The Chinese and Indians, despite having been brought here originally as indentured workers were never systematically and inhumanely deprived of their heritage and identity; only us Afrikans suffered such a wretched fate. Without an obstructive history, the Chinese and Indians have promoted themselves to join Europeans in the powerful class, while we Afrikans are still regulated to repeating the powerless class, which is the perceived criminal class.

The murders and gruesome crimes throughout the nation are for the most part black on black violence. Almost never are Europeans, Chinese or any other ethnicity not denied people the perpetrators or victims. They are also almost nonexistent in the nation jails and prisons. Blacks ram pack them and black warders guard them. All by design and plan, not accident or coincident. The truth is chattel slavery, colonialism and this here neo-colonialism are not separate, but succeeding parts of the one whole goal of our eternal damnation.

Emancipation did not come about because European had all of a sudden grown a conscience and recognized their evil or developed a good heart and sought repentance. In tandem with the granting of Independence, these decisions were merely strategic power-play necessities. No slaves were brought from Afrika - Afrikans we brought here and enslaved on plantations. These plantations were schools of horror. They did not impart knowledge but extracted it; nearly four hundred years of extraction. Extracting ourselves from us and us from our self. Extracting our education, our knowledge, our wisdom, our culture & heritage, our gods and spirituality, our sanity and identity. After been sufficiently emptied of Afrika and being (conscious) Afrikans, we were then deluged with Eurocentric ideals. Colonialism was the implanting of a new identity, a false identity, an anti-Afrikan, Eurocentric identity. Satisfied of us becoming phantoms, we were then granted Independence to showcase our adventures as roast breadfruit. Are you roast breadfruit, beloved students? If you are, you shall be no more. This is your epiphany. It matters not who has failed you or who is against you. The only concern is that you will not fail or be against yourself. You must make Afrika your best friend and favourite teacher. Be in love with Afrika and witness how much you love yourself and value others. See individualism and selfishness disappear as you revive your original Afrikan communal collective security spirit: "All for one. One for all. Working together in this manner we can know no failure", according to the wise guide of H.I.M. Emperor Haile Selassie I.

No more miseducation, no more own worst enemy, no more skylarking, no more ill-mannered behaviour, no more violence, no more decadence, no more taking for granted what our ancestors have killed, died and survived for, no more shame of Afrika, no more denying your Afrikan identity and power. The day is today and the time is now. You are your own masters, will you give yourself over to enslavement and colonisation or will you break free and empower yourself in the glory of your authenticity? Despite all the lies and demonic actions of white supremacy we are still Afrikans. A Chinese born anywhere in world but China is still Chinese, likewise a Japanese or a European or us Afrikans. We are not just descendants, we are Afrikans. The Nile still flows through your veins, beloved students. The secret of the pyramids is still within your DNA. To Know ThySelf - to recognize your divinity and be an asset, never a liability, is still your way of life. It's not too late, you are breathing.

Know yourself: conquer yourself and see the world becomes your clay as it did for your ancestors when they created the world's first and grandest nations. The probability to surpass said civilization lays latent within, beloved students, longing to burst forth and be the defining factor of your lives. Jamaica, your lives and the world will not get better without you harnessing your best you. The only way to the best you is an Afrikan centred conscious you - a Pan-Afrikan you. You must know and conquer yourselves. Begin now with the simple yet so vital, mastery of your breathing. Know the value of each inhale, feel its energy and know how to direct this energy where it's needed or where you want it. Get acquainted with meditation and yoga; get intimate with Afrika. Begin with the forming of an Afrikan (Cultural Renaissance) Club within the school. Kick start this effort with a library of Afrikan Centred Conscious Worldview books, films, documentaries and other educational resources. You are not alone; Afrikan clubs will soon be a norm of all schools. You are the fortunate first, smile and rise to the occasion. Greater is power within you than to be found anywhere in the world. You are not just boys and girls, you are all divine sparks of THE ALMIGHTY. Your Afrikan Club will have you recognize and behold this reality.

The mountain might be high and the road rugged but there is no obstacle your love and your strong and firm will cannot overcome. Be wholly committed to only what is good and best for you. Be mindful of the music you listen, the movies you watch, the books you read, the conversations you have, the food you eat, the thoughts you have, the company you keep, the words you speak, the future you are designing, be ever mindful. Be bold, be fearless, be confident. You are love and light. We love you and that is why we write to share with you the truth of the wealth within you. We are confident our effort is not in vain. You will reunite with your roots and grow strong and fruitful trees the marvel the world has not known for many centuries pass. Be of good-will and respectful to your teachers. They too are victims of the system but they bear the most sacred and challenging profession of all. They are all heroes. Do not make their job (their joy, it's the greatest joy for them to see you unearth your best) more difficult. Hands and heart, you and them in complete adherence to words of H.I.M. Emperor Haile Sellassie I and Mwalimu Marcus Garvey: "*A well organized education should not be one which prepares students for a good remuneration alone. It should be one that can help and guide them towards acquiring clear thinking, a fruitful mind, and an elevated spirit...To be learned in all that is worthwhile knowing. To store away in your head such facts as you need for the daily application of life, so that you may be better in all things, understand your fellowmen, and interpret your relation with your Creator. You can be educated in soul, vision as well as in mind. To see your enemy and know him is a part of your complete education; to spiritually regulate one's self is another of the higher form of education that fits you for a nobler place in life, and still, to approach your brother by the feeling of your own humanity, is an education that softens the ills of the world and makes us kind indeed."* It's all within your reach beloved students. No impossibility, no fairytale, by your will, there be a brighter day. Give thanks for the moment. Give thanks Word Sound Power. Give thanks for our ancestors. Love and thanks to you, Beautiful Ones.

Hotep

Ase'

Yours truly,

Namaste

www.ingramcontent.com/pod-product-compliance
Lightning Source LLC
Chambersburg PA
CBHW071737020426
42331CB00008B/2073